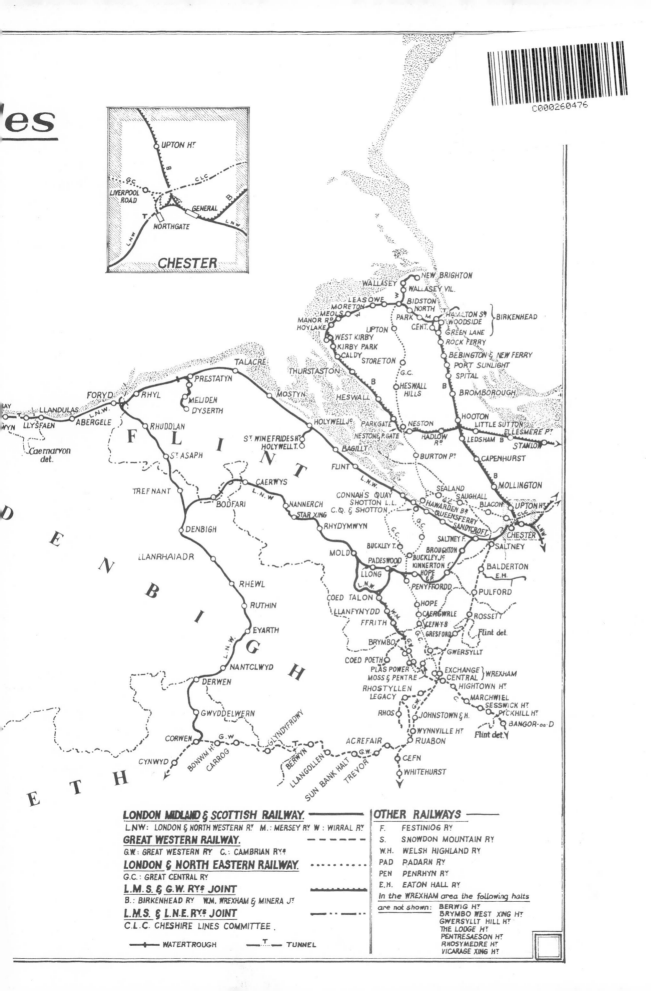

es

CHESTER

C000260476

LONDON MIDLAND & SCOTTISH RAILWAY. ————
L.NW: LONDON & NORTH WESTERN RY M.: MERSEY RY W: WIRRAL RY
GREAT WESTERN RAILWAY. – – – – –
G.W: GREAT WESTERN RY C.: CAMBRIAN RYS
LONDON & NORTH EASTERN RAILWAY. ··········
G.C.: GREAT CENTRAL RY
L.M.S. & G.W. RYS JOINT ———————
B.: BIRKENHEAD RY W.M. WREXHAM & MINERA JT
L.M.S. & L.N.E. RYS JOINT —·—·—·—
C.L.C. CHESHIRE LINES COMMITTEE.

—|—|— WATERTROUGH   —T— TUNNEL

OTHER RAILWAYS ————
F.   FESTINIOG RY
S.   SNOWDON MOUNTAIN RY
W.H. WELSH HIGHLAND RY
PAD   PADARN RY
PEN   PENRHYN RY
E.H. EATON HALL RY
In the WREXHAM area the following halts
are not shown: BERWIG HT
                BRYMBO WEST XING HT
                GWERSYLLT HILL HT
                THE LODGE HT
                PENTRESAESON HT
                RHOSYMEDRE HT
                VICARAGE XING HT

NORTH WALES STEAM (1927~1968)

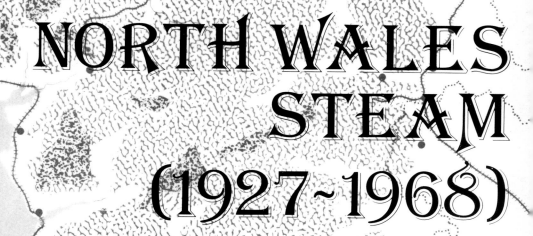

NORTH WALES STEAM (1927~1968)

by E.N. Kneale

Oxford Publishing Co.

FRONTISPIECE. A study in sheer elegance and grace. 'Royal Scot' No. 6159 photographed not many months after being built at the Hyde Park Works. She was later named *The Royal Air Force* and is seen here entering Bangor Tunnel with a Bangor–London Euston express.

H. A. Coulter

Working quite steadily up the gradient between Bethesda and Tregarth, 2–6–2T No. 41233 heads a Bethesda–Bangor goods alongside part of the Carneddi range of hills on a very overcast summer's day.

G. I. Davies

Copyright © Oxford Publishing Co. 1980

ISBN 0 86093 074 2
Reprinted 1986

Printed in Great Britain by
Biddles Ltd., Guildford and Kings Lynn.

Published by
Oxford Publishing Co.
Link House
West Street
Poole, Dorset

Dedication

To mothers and wives for infinite patience, and to railwaymen everywhere, who whether knowingly or not, have given so much pleasure to the enthusiast railway lover.

Acknowledgements

British Railways
(London Midland Region)
Mr. W. Jones
Mr. T. A. Jones
Mr. A. Jones
Mr. Manley Williams
Mr. J. Edwards
Mr. M. Catlin
Mr. B. Vernon

Mr. J. M. Lloyd
Mrs. Janet Owen
Mrs. Elizabeth Wood
Mr. E. Stanger
Mr. G. Jones
Mr. H. Martin
Mr. D. Fraser
Mr. R. Roberts

Introduction

The intention of this book is to portray in a pictorial manner the atmosphere and character of this main line in North Wales, and some of its branches during the Golden days of steam.

The period covered is from the late twenties to what is now generally considered to be the premature demise of the steam engine in the late sixties.

Few of us will deny the dignity of this most human-like of machines, whether it be a humble L&Y 0–6–0 coming to rest on Rhyl shed after a day's work, or the stirring sight of a 'Scot' leaning to the curve as it passes through the arch of the castle walls at Conway heading an up 'Irish Mail'.

All these once familiar sights, so much taken for granted, are alas no longer with us.

Today the journey between Chester and Holyhead is so much less interesting since the disappearance of the steam engine, which to sympathetic eyes seemed to enhance the natural beauty of the sea coast, mountain and valleys.

My sincere hope is that those who turn the pages of this book will pleasurably recall memories of a more colourful and less hurried era.

Finally, I must record my special gratitude to three friends and co-workers who in turn have been primarily responsible for the different periods in this collection: the late Mr. H. A. Coulter for pre-war items, Mr. H. Rogers-Jones for those of the post war decade; and my colleague Mr. B. A. Wynne for contributions of the remaining years.

E. N. Kneale
Menai Bridge
Anglesey

Rhagarweiniad

Amcan y llyfr hwn yw portreadu'n ddarluniadol nodweddion ac awyrgylch y brif linell hon yng Ngogledd Cymru a rhai o'i changhennau, yn ystod oes aur yr agerbeiriant.

Ymestyn y cyfnod a drafodir o ddiwedd yr ugeiniau hyd at yr hyn, a ystyrir bellach yn gyffredin, yn ddiwedd cyn-amserol y peiriant ager tua therfyn y chwedegau.

Ychydig ohonom y sydd na chydnabyddai urddas hwn, y mwyaf 'dynol' o'r peiriannau, boed L & Y 0–6–0 dinod yn dyfod i'w orffwysfa yn y sied yn y Rhyl ar ddiwedd ei ddiwrnod gwaith, neu gip gynhyrfiol ar Scot ar flaen Irish Mail yn gogwyddo tua'r tro wrth basio dan fwa muriau'r castell yng Nghonwy ar ei daith o Gaergybi.

Ond ysywaeth nid yw'r golygfeydd hyn, a fyddai mor gynefin gynt ac a gymerid mor ganiataol — nid ydynt mwyach gyda ni.

Heddiw, y mae'r daith o Gaer i Gaergybi yn llai ddiddorol er pan ddiflannodd y peiriant ager, a fyddai, i lygaid a adwaenai degwch, fel pe'n ychwanegu at brydferthwch naturiol traeth a mynydd a dyffryn.

Fy ngobaith diffuant yw y bydd i'r rhai a fydd yn troi dalennau'r llyfr hwn, y pleser o alw'n ôl atgofion am oes fwy lliwgar a chyfnod llai ei frys.

Yn olaf rhaid imi gofnodi fy niolch arbennig i dri chyfaill o gydweithwyr, a fu'n bennaf gyfrifol am y gwahanol gyfnodau yn y casgliad hwn; y diweddar Mr. H. A. Coulter am y cyfnod cyn y rhyfel, Mr. H. Rogers-Jones am y degawd wedi'r rhyfel, a'm cydweithiwr Mr. B. A. Wynne am gyfraniadau ynglŷn â'r blynyddoedd gweddill.

E.N. Kneale
Porth Aethwy
Ynys Môn

Plate 1. Framed by the unusual structure of Chester No. 6 box, ex Great Western 'Hall' Class locomotive No. 6947 *Helmingham Hall* appears out of the mistiness of a foggy morning running light engine from Mold Junction Shed.

E. N. Kneale

Chester

Gateway to North Wales

Plate 2. One of the busiest boxes at Chester was No. 6. Here the signalmen made the movements for the Great Western and London Midland trains. L.N.W. Rly and G.W. Rly block instruments can be seen side by side.

E. N. Kneale

Awaiting departure

Plate 3. A late summer's evening sees Black 5 No. 44819 passing beneath the L.N.W.R. signal gantry at Chester with a goods train for Mold Junction. Running light into Chester beside the old Great Western turntable is Black 5 No. 45002.

E. N. Kneale

Plate 4. 'Royal Scot' No. 6162 (un-named in the photograph, but later to become *Queen's Westminster Rifleman*), passes beneath the well-known L.N.W. Rly signal gantry at Chester with a down 'Irish Mail'.

H. A. Coulter

◁ *Plate 5*. Ex Fowler Class 4 2–6–4T No. 42350 moves out of Chester Station having previously brought in a train from Birkenhead. This class of locomotive was frequently seen along the coast during the summer service.

E. N. Kneale

◁ *Plate 6*. Chester as best remembered. Black 5 No. 45279 draws up to the end of the platform heading the Manchester to Holyhead express, whilst ex Great Western 'Castle' Class loco No. 5056 *Earl of Powis* is brought to a stand on the centre road.

E. N. Kneale

Plate 7. Black 5 No. 44859 heads a North Wales coast express out of Chester, whilst a Fairburn 2–6–4T shunts on one side of the Chester triangle.

E. N. Kneale

Plate 8. Great Western 'Hall' Class No. 4901 *Adderley Hall* departing from Chester at the head of a Birkenhead–Paddington express.

H. A. Coulter

Plate 9. Ex L.M.S. 2−6−0 Class 5 No. 42756 heads a relief train out of Chester.

Keith Smith

Plate 10. A down North Wales coast express, headed by 'Precursor' No. 5229 *Servia* blasts her way out of Chester past No. 6 box.

H. A. Coulter

Freight from Chester

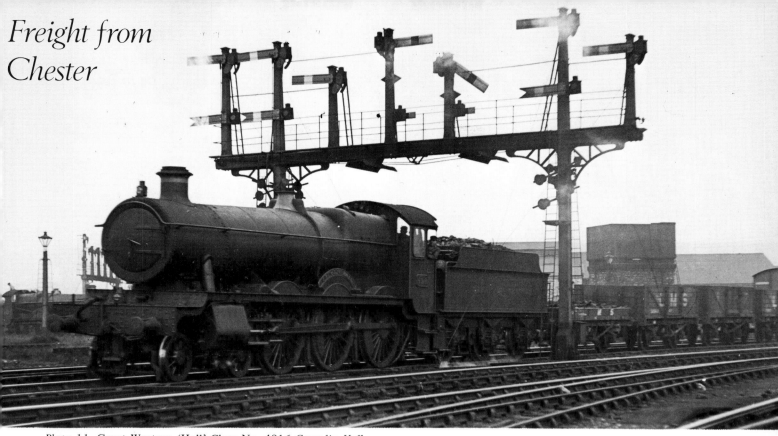

Plate 11. Great Western 'Hall' Class No. 4916 *Crumlin Hall* moves slowly out of Chester with a train of empty L.M.S. wagons.

H. A. Coulter

Plate 12. B.R. Class 5 No. 73040 on the down fast line rapidly overtakes ex W.D. 2–8–0 No. 90192 heading a mixed goods on the down slow line out of Chester.

Keith Smith

Mold
Junction

Plate 14. Ex L.M.S. Class 5 No. 42782 clanks slowly down the side of Mold Junction shed on its way to the goods yard. On shed can be seen a Saltley Black 5 No. 44775 and 8F 2–8–0 No. 48297 from Speke Junction.

E. N. Kneale

◁ *Plate 13.* Class 8F 2–8–0 No. 48741 runs slowly off the ash pit and prepares to take on coal at Mold Junction Depot.

B. A. Wynne

Plate 15. 'Hall' Class loco No. 6901 *Arley Hall* has the ash taken out of its smokebox on Mold Junction Shed.

B. A. Wynne

Plate 16. Black 5 No. 45495 with steam hissing from a leaking gland, heads an early morning goods into Mold Junction. Mold Junction was better known by railwaymen as 'Spike Island', which was derived from the spiked railing that surrounded the barracks and some of the railwaymen's houses.

B. A. Wynne

Plate 17. Re-built 'Scot' No. 46166 *London Rifle Brigade* of Carlisle Kingmoor draws into Mold Junction with an early morning goods.

B. A. Wynne

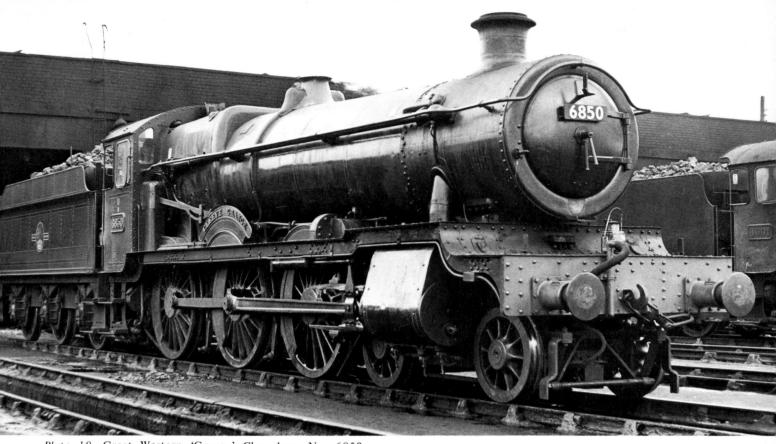

Plate 18. Great Western 'Grange' Class loco No. 6850 *Cleeve Grange* stands outside Mold Junction Shed. After the closure of the Great Western Shed at Chester, Mold Junction Shed stabled, over the years, many different classes of Great Western locomotives.

B. A. Wynne

Plate 19. Ex L.N.E.R. Bl 2–6–0 No. 61016 *Inyala* from Mirfield, Yorkshire, backs slowly off Mold Junction Shed, and on to the marshalling yard a little way down the line. She was seen later in the day heading a northern bound freight train through Chester.

B. A. Wynne

Through the border counties

Plate 20. Ex G.C. Rly 4–4–2T (L.N.E.R. Class C13 No. 5190) crosses Hawarden Bridge with a local train for Chester. *H. A. Coulter*

Plate 21. Ex G.C. Rly 4–4–2T (L.N.E.R. Class C13 No. 5455) is seen passing under a road bridge near Shotton at the head of a local train. *H. A. Coulter*

Plate 22. Ex L.N.W.R. 'Claughton' No. 5930 G. R. Jebb rushes past Mostyn heading the up 'Welshman' towards Chester and the South.

H. A. Coulter

Plate 23. Framed by one of the arches of a road bridge, Fairburn 4MT 2−6−4T No. 42198 heads its train from Rhyl towards Chester.

Keith Smith

Experimental designs

Plate 24. 'Royal Scot' Class No. 6100 *Royal Scot* seen here near Mostyn heading a down express to Holyhead. The small smoke deflectors on either side of her chimney are to help lift the exhaust away from the locomotive. Prior to a visit to the United States in the 30's, 6100 and 6152 changed names and numbers.

H. A. Coulter

Plate 25. During the early 30's various methods were tried by the L.M.S. to prevent steam and smoke drifting down the side of the boiler and so obscuring the vision of the driver and fireman. This photo shows 'Royal Scot' No. 6161 *King's Own* with a front end modification. The upper part of the smokebox has been cut away and a stovepipe chimney fitted. The cone-shaped protrusion and the projecting curved plate following the curvature of the smokebox were to effect an increase in air pressure as the loco was moving along, and so lift the exhaust well clear of the engine.

H.A. Coulter

Rhyl

Plate 26. Ex Midland 3F 0–6–0 locomotive No. 43618 rests on Rhyl Shed after a day's work.

B. A. Wynne

Plate 27. Ex L&Y 0–6–0 No. 52119 looking quite spick and span outside Rhyl Shed.

B. A. Wynne

Plate 28. Black 5 No. 45335 eases on to Rhyl turntable. In the background 'Jubilee' No. 45737 *Atlas* moves off the shed.

B. A. Wynne

Plate 29. B.R. Class 2MT 2–6–2T No. 41276 simmers gently at Rhyl, whilst waiting her turn of duty. This loco often worked the summer 'Welsh Dragon' service between Rhyl and Llandudno.

B. A. Wynne

Plate 30. Llandudno Junction Black 5 No. 45348 passes beneath the distinctive upper quadrant signal gantry to the east of Rhyl Station, with a stopping train for Chester.

Keith Smith

Plate 31. Black 5 No. 45446 shunting in the Rhyl goods yard on a very warm summer's afternoon.

E. N. Kneale

Colwyn Bay

Plate 33. Stanier Pacific No. 46222 *Queen Mary* being admired by some young boys at Colwyn Bay Station. She was obliged to take the down slow line whilst heading a down 'Irish Mail'.

E. N. Kneale

◁ Plate 32. 'Jubilee' Class No. 45640 *Frobisher* receives a final oiling prior to heading a Manchester train from Rhyl.

B. A. Wynne

Plate 34. A Llandudno–Manchester express departing from Colwyn Bay Station headed by Black 5 No. 45311. Some of the tallest signal posts on this line were once seen here on the up and down fast lines, so that the drivers could sight the arms above the station building as they rounded the curve.

E. N. Kneale

Plate 35. With home and distant signals off, Black 5 No. 45243 passes by Colwyn Bay No. 1 box and heads towards the station with a Manchester–Llandudno express.

E. N. Kneale

Plate 37. Re-built 'Royal Scot' No. 46150 *The Life Guardsman* makes her departure from Llandudno Junction Station on a ▷ bright, but very cold winter's morning, for Holyhead. The raked-out ash beneath the brazier, to stop the water column freezing up, bears evidence of a keen frost during the previous night.

H. Rogers Jones

Plate 36. A Stanier Class 5 with Caprotti gear, No. 44740 climbs the 1:300 gradient from Colwyn Bay to the Llandulas tunnel after which it will have a fast run down the falling gradient to Abergele. Across the bay on the right is the Little Orme near Llandudno.

H. Rogers Jones

Llandudno
Junction

Plate 38. An immaculately clean 'Patriot' Class locomotive No. 45509 *The Derbyshire Yeomanry* moves slowly out of Llandudno Junction Station heading the 9.10 a.m. Llandudno–London Euston express. The engines on this turn hauled the 2.38 p.m. Crewe–Holyhead returning with a parcels train, which arrived back in the Junction around 9.30 p.m. The following morning it would move off the shed at 7.25 and either work empty stock, or travel light engine to Llandudno. Junction men then worked this loco as far as Crewe, at which point they were relieved and the train continued on to London.

H. Rogers Jones

Plate 39. Re-built 'Scot' No. 46129 *The Scottish Horse* approaches Llandudno Junction with an express from the North.

H. Rogers Jones

Plate 40. Un-named 'Claughton' No. 5989 passes sister engine No. 5926 *Sir Herbert Walker K.C.B.* with a Manchester–Holyhead express between Llandudno Junction and Conwy.

H. A. Coulter

◁ *Plate 41.* Cleaning out ash pits was one of many unpleasant and rather mundane jobs that had to be done on a loco shed, possibly made even less attractive, as seen in this picture. On a wet Monday morning, Black 5 No. 44821 waits to run on to the pit prior to having her fire cleaned on Llandudno Junction Shed.

E. N. Kneale

Plate 42. The 'intruders'. Hunslet diesel shunter No. D2607 and companion stand alongside Holyhead's Black 5 No. 45247 on Llandudno Junction Shed.

E. N. Kneale

Plate 43. B.R. Class 5 No. 73025 receiving a mileage overhaul on Llandudno Junction Shed. The wheels are from Black 5 No. 45206 which is just out of the picture.

B. A. Wynne

Plate 44. Stanier 8F 2–8–0 No. 48648 on Llandudno Junction Shed. The hydraulic press seen in the foreground was used for pressing out worn bushes.

B. A. Wynne

Plate 45. The morning after. The two locomotives that were involved in the tragic accident at Penmaenmawr now stand ▷ almost as they had collided on the back road of Llandudno Junction Shed. On the left of the picture is the damaged tender of the Class 5 2–6–0 loco No. 42885, and to the right the crumpled front end, minus the front bogies, of re-built 'Royal Scot' No. 46119 *Lancashire Fusilier*.

H. Rogers Jones

Plate 46. Two blazing braziers on a freezing day provide cold comfort indeed for a condemned B.R. Class 2 tank engine on ▷ Llandudno Junction Shed.

E. N. Kneale

Llandudno Branch

Plate 48. A very popular train during the days of steam was the 9.10 a.m. from Llandudno to Euston. Here rebuilt 'Scot' No. 46134 *The Cheshire Regiment* pulls away from Deganwy, an attractive little resort between Llandudno and Llandudno Junction.

H. Rogers Jones

◁ Plate 47. Looking towards Llandudno Junction locomotive and carriage sheds from the platform end on a raw but sunny winter's morning, an unidentified 4–4–0 2P pushes a Black 5 and a 2–6–4T towards the coaling shed. The last Llandudno Junction 4–4–0 2P was No. 40635, which was an ex S&D.J.R. engine.

H. Rogers Jones

Plate 49. Derailment at Deganwy. An ex L.N.W.R. 2–4–2T is seen here being helped back on to the road.

H. A. Coulter

Llandudno

◁ *Plate 50.* The bright winter sun dramatically catches the exhaust steam and smoke from re-built 'Scot' No. 46131 *The Royal Warwickshire Regiment* as she heads her London bound train out of Deganwy Station on a crisp December morning.

H. Rogers Jones

Plate 51. Ex L.N.W.R. 4–4–0 'George the Fifth' Class No. 25376 *Snipe* on Llandudno turntable.

H. A. Coulter

Plate 52. A typical Saturday scene at Llandudno during the summer holiday period. A Class 5 sets off with a special to Derby. The engine on the left is going onto the turntable, after which it will have its fire cleaned and take on water at the tower. The three in the centre are waiting for a clear road to Llandudno Junction for coaling etc. They will return light engine or with empty stock to Llandudno for their journey back to the Midlands and the North.

H. Rogers Jones

Blaenau ffestiniog Branch

Plate 53. The beauty and gentleness of the Lledr Valley in high summer is captured in this study of an Ivatt 2MT winding its way along the branch line towards Roman Bridge, with its two-coach train for Blaenau Ffestiniog.

H. Rogers Jones

Plate 54. On a rather dull summer's afternoon Stanier Class 3MT 2–6–2T No. 40130 approaches Tal-y-Cafn Station with the 3.5 p.m., Llandudno Junction–Blaenau Ffestiniog local train. On the left of the picture is part of the Afon Conwy, where salmon are netted in large numbers. Hidden behind the trees on the right are the famous Bodnant Gardens, now part of the National Trust.

H. Rogers Jones

Plate 55. This is typical of the scenery in the Conwy Valley where in many parts the railway keeps close company with the river, in this case the Conwy. The Ivatt 2–6–2T No. 40208 coasts smoothly down towards Betws-y-Coed after leaving Llanrwst. Across the river are the Clwyd Hills of Denbighshire.

H. Rogers Jones

Plate 56. Harvest time in the Lledr Valley. In the autumn this branch line from Llandudno Junction to Blaenau Ffestiniog is one of the most picturesque in the whole country. The great variety of trees and mown fields provides a glorious patchwork of colour. The train is seen here coasting down the steep gradients between Pont-y-Pant (The Bridge in the Hollow), and Betws-y-Coed (Chapel in the Woods). 'Betws' originated from the old English 'Bede-House'.

H. Rogers Jones

Plate 57. An Ivatt Class 2MT gathers speed to tackle the steep gradients and tight curves in the Lledr Valley, seen here crossing Gethin's Bridge which spans the Afon Lledr and the road leading up to the Crimea Pass. The bridge was so named after the builder who lived in the district and employed local labour.

H. Rogers Jones

Plate 58. The 3.56 p.m. Llandudno Junction to Blaenau Ffestiniog, seen on a summer afternoon between Pont-y-Pant and Dolwyd-delan. After parting from Afon Conwy at Betws-y-Coed the rail-way now meanders along the banks of Afon Lledr. The 'Af' in Afon (River) is pronounced as the 'Av' as in the English word 'have', not as Shakespeare's Avon.

H. Rogers Jones

Plate 59. Clouds begin to gather and encroach upon the mountainside at Blaenau Ffestiniog as Black 5 No. 44711, which has just finished shunting duties, makes its way home to Llandudno Junction.

E. N. Kneale

West from
Llandudno Junction
Conwy

Plate 61. 'Royal Scot' No. 6139 *The Welch Regiment* leans to the curve at Conwy with a Bangor–London express.

H. A. Coulter

◁ Plate 60. 'Fairburn' 2–6–4T No. 42261 approaches the archway in the castle wall prior to entering Conwy Station.

H. A. Coulter

Plate 62. The up 'Irish Mail' emerging from the tunnel at the west end of Conwy Station, drawn by 'Britannia' No. 70049, later named *Solway Firth*. Note the curved sided tender (Class BR1D), one of only nine fitted to these fine locomotives. This tunnel carries a road and part of the old town walls.

H. Rogers Jones

Plate 63. Beside the castle and above the bowling green at Conwy, an ex W.D. 2-8-0 No. 90227 ambles towards the Conwy tubular bridge and Llandudno Junction on a late summer's afternoon with a long train of empty wagons.

H. Rogers Jones

Plate 64. Emerging on the down line to Holyhead, re-built 'Scot' No. 46101 *Royal Scots Grey* is dwarfed by the imposing western portals of Conwy Tubular Bridge, designed by Francis Thompson to harmonise with the centuries-old castle. The limestone facings were quarried from Penmon Point in Anglesey, and also from the Great Orme. The first tube was raised in January, 1848, under the supervision of the engineer Robert Stephenson.

H. Rogers Jones

Plate 65. Where the mountains sweep down to the sea. An unidentified 'Prince of Wales' locomotive emerges at the head of a down North Wales coast express, from the avalanche shelter at Pen-y-Clip, between Conwy and Penmaenmawr.

H. A. Coulter

Plate 67. Re-built 'Scot' No. 46156 *The South Wales Borderer* makes a rapid departure from Penmaenmawr Station with a down semi fast express for Holyhead. ▷

Keith Smith

Plate 68. Specials meet at Penmaenmawr. ▷ Black 5 No. 45225 moves away from the up platform with a train for the North, whilst No. 45345 prepares to enter the station at the head of a special from Liverpool.

E. N. Kneale

Plate 66. 'Experiment' Class loco No. 5472 heads a train towards Llandudno Junction near the Pen-y-Clip viaduct. The tower and overhead cables were part of the road construction operation that was in progress at that time, around 1934.

H. A. Coulter

Penmaenmawr

The Penmaenmawr accident

Plate 69

Plate 70. General scene of destruction to some of the carriages. The last three coaches though slightly derailed stayed in an upright position.

A. Pratt

Plate 71

Llanfairfechan

Plate 72. 'Prince of Wales' Class No. 5687 *Hotspur* shuts off steam and coasts towards Llanfairfechan Station under the massive backdrop of Penmaenmawr Mountain. It is interesting to note that the first coach is of ex Caledonian stock. Shortly after the amalgamation of the many companies into the 'big four', a number of these carriages found their way into North Wales.

H. A. Coulter

◁ Plate 69. As the heavy lifting steam cranes clear the wreckage from the up and down lines, ex L.M.S. 8F 2–8–0 No. 48296 has run tender first from Llandudno Junction and attached itself to the light engine, ex L.M.S. Class 5 2–6–0 No. 42885. After being pulled clear of the Scot, the tender of the Class 5 was re-railed and the loco with tender attached towed to the Junction. The re-built 'Scot' was eventually re-railed and also towed to Llandudno Junction, but minus her front bogies.

A. Pratt

◁ Plate 71. One of the two heavy lifting cranes that were brought to the scene of the accident takes the strain and gently begins to lift one of the carriages clear of the line. The Great Orme of Llandudno can be seen in the background.

A. Pratt

Plate 73. 'Royal Scot' No. 6169 *The Boy Scout* rushes past the village of Llanfairfechan with a down 'Irish Mail'. Penmaenmawr Mountain can be seen in the background.

H. A. Coulter

Penrhyn

◁ *Plate 74.* 'Precursor' Class No. 25310 *Thunderer* by name and by the way she is working, by nature, heads a Bangor to Liverpool special, near Aber.

H. A. Coulter

◁ *Plate 75.* 'Time for tea'. A permanent way workman looks back towards his workmates with a billy of tea from the footplate of a Black 5 No. 44821. It was a Sunday morning working putting down fresh ballast on the up line between Gypsy Corner and Aber Troughs.

B. A. Wynne

Plate 76. Rebuilt 'Claughton' No. 6029 picking up speed as she passes Port Penrhyn siding signal box with an up 'Irish Mail'.

H. A. Coulter

Plate 77. Making up lost time, Black 5 No. 44863 blasts its way past Penrhyn siding box and on towards Chester with an express for Crewe. The lines leading to the siding can be seen, and also a small branch line from here led to Port Penrhyn.

G. I. Davies

Plate 79. Bangor's station pilot sets back onto a Chester parcels train. Note the peculiar head code for a station pilot.

B. A. Wynne

Plate 78. Approaching Bangor Station from the eastern end, Fairburn 4MT 2–6–4T No. 42286 brings her train into the station out of the darkness of Belmont Tunnel with a Caernarfon-Rhyl (S.O.) train.

E. N. Kneale

Plate 80. A damp and miserable dull November morning is brightened by an unusual visitor bringing into Bangor a Chester parcels train. Ex L.M.S. 4MT 2–6–4T No. 42350 passes the signals at the end of the Bethesda branch bay and into the platform.

E. N. Kneale

Plate 82. Re-built 'Royal Scot' No. 46152 *The King's Dragoon Guardsman* propels empty coaching stock towards the cross-over at the western end of Bangor Station. They will then be drawn forward into No. 1 platform and become the relief coaches for the 12.50 p.m. London train.

B. A. Wynne

◁ Plate 81. The fireman of re-built 'Scot' No. 46152 gives the glass protector a final rub before entering Bangor tunnel with an express for Manchester.

E. N. Kneale

Plate 83. Stanier 'Coronation' Pacific No. 46224 *Princess Alexandra* takes the avoiding line through Bangor. North Wales only occasionally saw Scottish Pacifics, but when they did come, they were always in immaculate condition. As can be seen by her shed plate, No. 46224 was from Polmadie (Glasgow).

B. A. Wynne

Plate 85. The Amlwch 'push and pull' having brought its train into Bangor Station headed by B.R. 2MT 2–6–2T No. 84003, now gently pushes the two-coach train out of the station and towards No. 2 Box where she will be crossed over to one of the down platforms, and await her next turn of duty to Amlwch.

E. N. Kneale

◁ *Plate 84.* With a heavy train behind her, Fairburn 4MT 2–6–4T No. 42282 plunges into the already smoke laden tunnel and leaves a sunny afternoon behind, albeit for a short period of time.

E. N. Kneale

Plate 86. Bangor Station reverberates to the sound of tank engines as some arrive and others take their leave. Stanier 4MT 2–6–4T No. 42488 moves very slowly up the platform after having brought in a Chester parcels train. Ahead of it Ivatt 2MT 2–6–2T No. 41226 prepares to propel the Amlwch push and pull away from the station. Arriving alongside the up platform, a Butlins special from Pwllheli, double headed by Fairburn and Stanier tank engines Nos. 42074 and 42478, their motions almost identically placed, pass beneath the enclosed footbridge and prepare to come to a stand at the eastern end of the station.

E. N. Kneale

Plate 87. A quiet summer's afternoon at the end of Bangor's No. 3 platform, sees the driver of Ivatt 2MT 2-6-2T No. 41226 steadying the leather water bag with his foot as he allows water from the tower to fill the tanks of his engine.

E. N. Kneale

Plate 88. The fireman of B.R. Pacific No. 70051 *Firth of Forth* climbs down from the footplate to walk across the lines and into Bangor No. 1 signal box to comply with Rule 55.

E. N. Kneale

Plate 89. Blowing off with a deafening roar and with its right hand side injector overflowing, B.R. Pacific No. 70046 *Anzac* heads the 'Horse and Carriage' past Bangor No. 2 box and on towards Chester.

B. A. Wynne

Plate 90. Storming out of Bangor Station, Stanier 4MT 2–6–4T No. 42478 makes for the tunnel with a Bangor–Pwllheli train sending up an impressive exhaust on a rather overcast summer's day.

E. N. Kneale

Plate 91. On a dull November morning, Stanier Pacific No. 46251 *City of Nottingham* brings the Holyhead 'Horse and Carriage' past Bangor No. 1 box and stops just short of the tunnel entrance. Some of these trains were of such length as to block the crossover at the eastern end of the Station.

E. N. Kneale

Bangor shed

Plate 93. Class 4F 0–6–0 No. 44389 waiting her turn to run off the shed whilst a Fairburn 2–6–4T No. 42074 prepares to take on water.

B. A. Wynne

◁ *Plate 92.* Stanier Pacific No. 46248 *City of Leeds* ambles through Bangor Station past Black 5 No. 45091 on its way, with a parcels train, towards Chester.

B. A. Wynne

Plate 94. Ex War Department locomotive 2–8–0 8F No. 90264 resting on Bangor Shed after having brought down an out of gauge train earlier in the day.

B. A. Wynne

Plate 95. Only the gentle hiss of steam breaks the silence of a Sunday afternoon on Bangor Shed. Some are strangers that have worked specials down the previous day.

E. N. Kneale

Plate 96. Black 5 for the Royal Train at Bangor Shed. It is interesting to note that the front couplings have been removed for cleaning.

B. A. Wynne

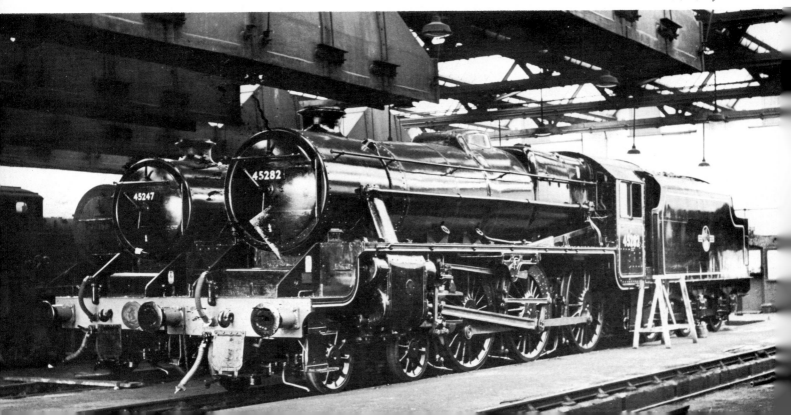

Plate 97. 'Jubilee' Class 4–6–0 No. 45608 *Gibraltar* seen on a warm summer's afternoon backing slowly off from the coaling stage, before running light engine towards Chester.

B. A. Wynne

Plate 98. Ex L&Y 0–6–0 No. 52230 backing on to Bangor Shed after a day's hard work.

L. V. Williams

Plate 99. One of the Bangor shed fitters, watched by the engine driver, makes minor adjustments to a cylinder relief valve on Black 5 No. 45328. Today, no doubt, fitters would have torches or electric light to do such work, but not so when this photograph was taken in the 60's. There was just an oil lamp, seen bottom right-hand side of picture.

E. N. Kneale

Plate 100. In the quiet of a late summer's evening, a lone fireman tends his lamps in preparation for a late turn. The special reporting number boards leaning against the wall bear evidence of a very busy summer Saturday at Bangor.

E. N. Kneale

Plate 101. There cannot have been many sheds in the U.K. during the 60's that still depended upon men to hand-coal locomotives. Bangor shed was one of them. The picture shows a coaler throwing lumps into the tender of B.R. Pacific No. 70029 *Shooting Star.*

E. N. Kneale

Pre-Nationalisation

Plate 102. Ex L.N.W.R. Bowen Cooke 4–6–2T No. 6965 being prepared by her fireman and driver for a turn to Afon Wen on a particularly misty morning at Bangor.

H. A. Coulter

Plate 103. An ex L.N.W.R. 0–6–0 No. 8540 known as 'Cauliflowers', rests after a day's work on Bangor Shed. Part of an ex L.N.W.R. 0–6–2 coal side tank can be seen ahead of her.

H. A. Coulter

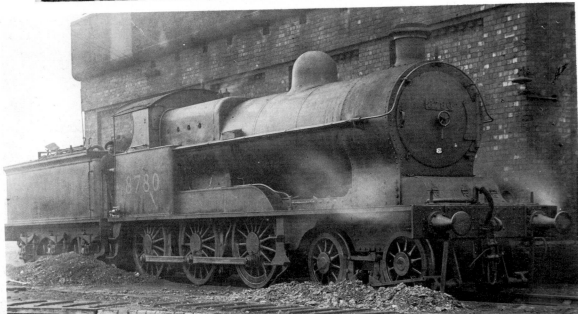

Plate 104. 'Royal Scot' No. 6101 *Royal Scots Grey* on Bangor Shed taken shortly after she was built. It is interesting to note the front bogie brakes, which were later discarded.

H. A. Coulter

Plate 105. 'Royal Scot' No. 6157 *The Royal Artilleryman* having its smokebox cleaned out and tubes brushed on Bangor Shed.

H.A. Coulter

Plate 106. An ex L.N.W.R. goods or mixed traffic locomotive No. 8780, having its fire dropped on Bangor Shed. An unusual feature of this locomotive is the front bogie braking system.

H. A. Coulter

Plate 107. 'Royal Scot' Class No. 6152 *The King's Dragoon Guardsman* seen here acting as Royal Engine on the occasion of the visit of King George VI, Queen Elizabeth, and the Princesses Elizabeth and Margaret Rose to Bangor, in July 1937.

H. A. Coulter

Plate 108. 'Royal Scot' No. 6162 *Queen's Westminster Rifleman* (seen here before she was named) bursts into the sunlight from the gloom of Belmont Tunnel, Bangor, with a down 'Irish Mail'.

H. A. Coulter

Freight from Bangor

Plate 110. A powerful engine for a heavy load in the form of B.R. 9F No. 92127. This was a Sunday morning 'wrong line' working, as the permanent way men were working on the up fast line.

B. A. Wynne

◁ *Plate 109.* A Class 4F 0–6–0 L.M.S. goods engine No. 4369 emerges from Bangor Tunnel and makes her way towards Menai Bridge goods yards, where she will pick up more wagons and take them across Anglesey to Holyhead.

H. A. Coulter

Plate 111. An ex works Stanier Class 8F 2–8–0 No. 48749 brings a mixed goods through Bangor Station and passes Black 5 No. 44807 which has just brought in the Chester parcels train.

E. N. Kneale

Plate 112. The Cambrian Radio Cruise Train headed by Great Western Collett 0–6–0 No. 3202 passes Bethesda Junction signal box en route from Rhyl to Barmouth and Aberdovey.

G. I. Davies

Plate 113. 'Royal Scot' No. 6161 *King's Own* gets hold of an up 'Irish Mail' as it passes Bethesda Junction signal box.

H.A. Coulter

Plate 114. Backing out of the Bethesda Station loop line on a bright winter's morning, Ivatt 2MT 2–6–2T No. 41324 prepares to shunt in the station yard.

G. I. Davies

Bethesda

Plate 115. B.R. Class 2MT No. 78058 runs tender first, light engine, between Glasynfryn and Bethesda Junction.

B. A. Wynne

Bangor to Caernarfon

Plate 116. One of Bangor's ex L.N.W.R. 0–6–2Ts, known as "Coal side tanks", rushes out of one of the twin bores of Treborth Tunnel on its way to Caernarfon with a local from Bangor.

H. A. Coulter

Plate 117. A Llandudno Junction Black 5 No. 45282 opens up for the rising gradient between Nant y Garth, where this photograph was taken, and Treborth Station with a train of old sleepers from Caernarfon Station.

B. A. Wynne

Plate 118. Ex L&Y 0–6–0 No. 52119 hoists a canopy of smoke over Port Siding signal box, whilst working very hard haul-ing a maximum load of 16 wagons of slate up the 1:40 incline from the quay side at Port Dinorwic. These loads were always worked tender first towards Bangor because of the narrow bore of Treborth Tunnel. Even going into the tunnel in this way, the fireman and engine driver would on occasions be forced down on to their hands and knees trying to get fresh air.

R. Owen

Plate 119. Llanberis pick up goods headed by Fairburn 2–6–4T No. 42209 passes Port Dinorwic Station on its way back to Menai Bridge goods yard.

B. A. Wynne

Caernarfon

Plate 120. Stanier 4MT 2–6–4T No. 42482 stands at the head of a Caernarfon–Chester (S.O.) passenger train. The platform which she is alongside, is made of timber, and was specially constructed as an extra platform to cope with the many extra trains that ran into Caernarfon during the Investiture of the Prince of Wales in 1911. It became known to some as the King Edward Platform. Running down the middle road is a Llanberis to Menai Bridge goods train headed by 2–6–4T No. 42489.

B. A. Wynne

Plate 121. On a warm Saturday afternoon Black 5 No. 45237 comes to a stand in Caernarfon Station with a special from Manchester.

E. N. Kneale

Plate 122. On a very wet and miserable day, Ivatt 2MT 2–6–2T No. 41234 brings into Caernarfon Station the last steam hauled passenger train from Afon Wen to Bangor. One of the national emblems of Wales, the three feathers and motto 'Ich Dien', can be seen on the facing wall of the station house.

E. N. Kneale

Plate 123. A summer holiday special enters Caernarfon Station from the North, headed by Black 5 No. 45113, to be met by friends and relatives. The d.m.u. on the opposite platform waits for the signal prior to leaving for Bangor.

E. N. Kneale

Plate 124. Fairburn 4MT 2–6–4T No. 42283 takes on water at Caernarfon.

E. N. Kneale

Plate 125. B.R. Class 4 No. 75009 waits patiently beside Caernarfon No. 2 box before running light engine to Llanberis.

E. N. Kneale

Plate 126. The beginning of the end for Caernarfon. The Caernarfon–Afon Wen line has been closed, and so signal gantrys have to be lifted, and possibly used elsewhere, and also some of the track. Black 5 No. 45325 with the steam crane and attendant stock complete the operation.

E. N. Kneale

Plate 128. A warm summer's afternoon sees Black 5 No. 45298 heading a train of empties slowly up the incline between Pont Rhythallt and Caernarfon on the Llanberis Branch.

B. A. Wynne

◁ *Plate 127.* B.R. Class 4 No. 75009 pulls away from Cwm-y-Glo with a train of mixed stock from Llanberis and heads towards Pont Rhythallt Station and Caernarfon.

E. N. Kneale

Plate 129. High summer at Llanberis. The Bangor to Llanberis pick up goods simmers at the end of the platform whilst the crew and station officials talk together beneath the station awning. The tower of Dolbadarn Castle can be seen on the left of the guard's van.

B. A. Wynne

Caernarfon to Afon Wen

Plate 130. Early morning workmen's train headed by B.R. Class 2 tender engine No. 78058, enters Pen-y-Groes with a stopping train from Afon Wen to Bangor.

B. A. Wynne

Plate 131. Fairburn 4MT 2–6–4T No. 42209 waits for the signal at Pen-y-Groes. The home signal that can be seen on the left of the picture is for the Nantlle Vale Branch.

B. A. Wynne

Plate 132. Fairburn 4MT 2—6—4T No. 42209 on a Bangor to Afon Wen pick up goods, stops at the end of Brynkir Station to take on water.

B. A. Wynne

Plate 133. Shunting at Afon Wen with Fairburn 4MT 2—6—2T No. 42202. This is a small part of the ex 2.16 a.m., Liverpool–Bangor goods train.

B. A. Wynne

Menai Tubular Bridge

Plate 134. With steam shut off, 'Royal Scot' No. 6161 *King's Own* passes between the lions that stand guard at the approaches to the Tubular Bridge, before plunging, with whistle sounding, into the down tube on the last leg of a journey from London to Holyhead.

H. A. Coulter

Plate 135. An unidentified 'Precursor' approaches the picturesque setting to the Tubular Bridge with a semi-fast express. The Snowdonian range can be seen in the background.

H. A. Coulter

Plate 136. A relief 'Irish Mail' hauled by an unidentified 'Midland Compound' and a 'Claughton', swings round the tight curve as they come off the Tubular Bridge and make their way towards London.   H. A. Coulter

Plate 137. Ex L.M.S. Class 2MT 2–6–2T No. 41233 comes off the Britannia Bridge heading an Amlwch goods towards Bangor.

E. N. Kneale

*On into
Anglesey...*

menai Bridge Station

Menai Bridge staff

Plate 140. Late evening entry. The rays of a setting sun soften the inside of Menai Bridge box, and cast long shadows as the signalman enters the time of a passing local train for Caernarfon.

E. N. Kneale

◁ *Plate 138.* L.M.S. 2–6–2T No. 79 departs from Menai Bridge Station with a Bangor to Pwllheli local train.

H. A. Coulter

◁ *Plate 139.* A scene typical of many small Welsh country stations. B.R. Class 2MT No. 78059 shunts in the station yard. Later she will run light engine to the larger goods yard, the cabins of which can be seen in the background, and marshall the evening's Menai Bridge to Mold Junction goods.

E. N. Kneale

Plate 141. Time off to roll a cigarette and reminisce about railways in times gone by.

E. N. Kneale

Menai Woods

Plate 142. A classic combination with 'Precursor' No. 5216 *Herald* and un-named 'Claughton' No. 5953, their rhythmic exhausts echoing around Menai Woods, picking up speed as they haul an up relief 'Irish Mail' to London Euston.

H. A. Coulter

Plate 143. On a late summer's evening re-built 'Scot' No. 46150 drifts round the curve leading out of Menai Woods with the last portion of a London Euston to Holyhead train.

E. N. Kneale

Plate 144. Stranger in the camp. Ex G.W.R. Collett 0−6−0 No. 3208 became Llandudno Junction's snowplough engine for the winter of 1962–63. She is seen here passing Llanfair P.G., Anglesey, after steaming up and down the Amlwch Branch to keep it open. She had originally come from Machynlleth Depot.

B. A. Wynne

Plate 145. Rushing beneath one of the many small road bridges that cross the main line on Anglesey, Stanier Pacific No. 46248 *City of Leeds*, double headed with Black 5 No. 45189, approaches Llanfair P.G. with an up relief 'Irish Mail'.

E. N. Kneale

Plate 146. During the early 60's, work started on renewing the timber sleepers in the 'up' tube of the Britannia Bridge, and consequently single line working came into operation between Llanfair P.G. and Menai Bridge. 'Coronation' Pacific No. 46240 *City of Coventry* has been brought to a stand by Llanfair P.G. home signal, the fireman has climbed down and walked to the box to receive the single line token, the signal has been pulled off, and the fireman waits for the driver of No. 46240 to draw forward and pick him up.

B. A. Wynne

Plate 147. Sunday morning work re-laying part of the down line between Llanfair P.G. and Gaerwen brings out a full squad of gangers and permanent way workers to finish the job in the limited time given. Black 5 No. 45413 stands by to propel the re-laying machine when required.

E. N. Kneale

Plate 148. Gaerwen in the rain. A miserable Monday evening with Ivatt 2MT 2–6–2T No. 41226 waiting to take the 6 o'clock push and pull to Amlwch. Even in 1963 oil lamps were still used to illuminate the platform and buildings at night. Three of them are shown in this photograph.

Keith Smith

Plate 149. As an unidentified Black 5 departs from Gaerwen Station with a Bangor to Holyhead stopping train, the driver of the Amlwch push and pull waits for the signalman in No. 1 box to open the crossing gates allowing his train to cross over from the up line to the down line, and pick up parcels that have been left on the platform and travellers for all stations to Amlwch. The photo was taken from the auto coach.

E. N. Kneale

Red Wharf Bay Branch

Plate 150. Although this picture was taken on the Red Wharf Bay branch long before the period this book covers, it was felt to be worthy of inclusion. It shows a contractor's locomotive on the branch during the building of the line around 1908.

Courtesy of Mr. H. Jones
Bodorgan

Plate 151. This photograph, taken in July 1908, shows the opening of the line with a view of what must be the majority of the local community, at Pentraeth Station. The locomotive is a L.N.W.R. 2–4–0 tank.

Courtesy of Miss Mary Parry

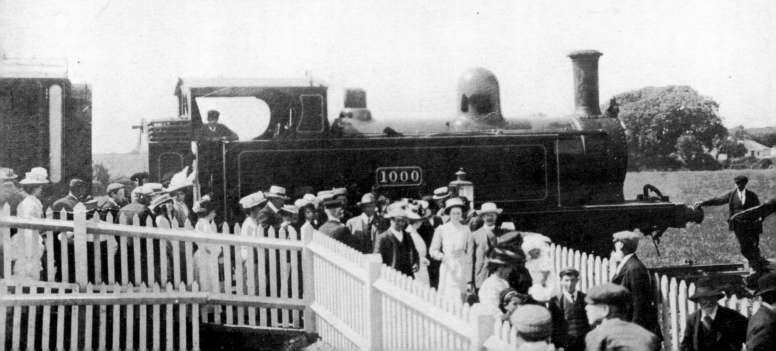

Plate 152. Sunshine and shadow on the Amlwch branch. Class 2MT 2–6–2T No. 41200 drifts down the bank between Holland Arms and Gaerwen with an Amlwch to Bangor goods.

B. A. Wynne

Plate 153. Clearance trials on the Amlwch branch. Stanier Class 4MT 2–6–4T No. 42606 runs very slowly through Llangefni Station watched critically by three members of the engineering department. The trials were successfully completed, and within a year Black 5s were allowed up the branch, and much later English Electric type 4 diesel locomotives were frequently seen.

E. N. Kneale

Amlwch Branch

Plate 154. B.R. Class 4MT No. 75009 spreads a mantle of exhaust over Amlwch Village as she leaves the station on a bitterly cold November afternoon with a train of chemical tanks.

E. N. Kneale

Plate 155. Whilst B.R. 2MT 2–6–2T No. 41234 performs shunting duties outside the goods shed, B.R. Class 2 No. 84003 backs into Amlwch Station after having taken on water further up the branch.

E. N. Kneale

...and on to Holyhead

Plate 156. Ex L.N.W.R. 'Claughton' No. 5926 *Sir Herbert Walker K.C.B.* heads a Chester to Holyhead local stopping train into Bodorgan Station.

H. A. Coulter

Plate 157. Drifting into Bodorgan Station on a warm summer's afternoon, Black 5 No. 45493 prepares to stop with a special for Holyhead.

B. A. Wynne

Plate 158. One of the most open stretches of line on Anglesey is between Ty Croes and Bodorgan. Here the full force of the prevailing south-westerly winds could make life, to say the least, uncomfortable on the footplate of an engine. Black 5 No. 45110 is seen here battling with such a wind, heading a cattle train towards Chester on a late winter's afternoon.

E. N. Kneale

Plate 159. A Holyhead to Chester passenger train enters Ty Croes Station on a summer's day headed by Black 5 No. 45277.

B. A. Wynne

Plate 160. Black 5 No. 44711 heads a train of empty flats past Ty Croes signal box.

B. A. Wynne

Plate 161. A fine study of this most versatile of locomotives. Black 5 No. 44821 comes to a stand at Ty Croes Station.

B. A. Wynne

holyhead ~ *The end of the line*

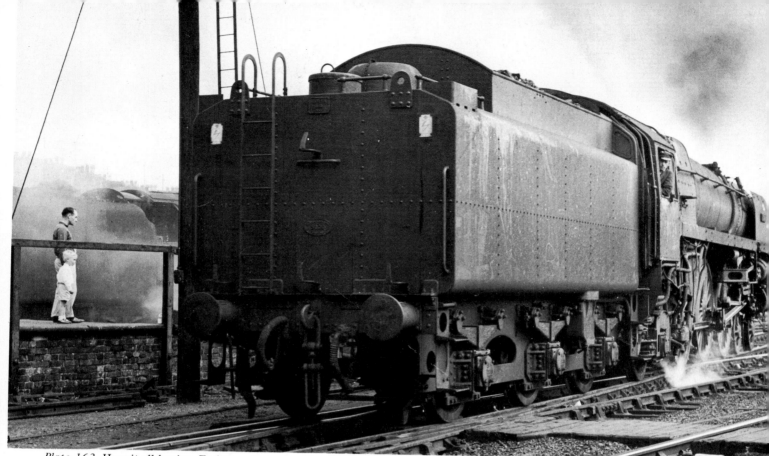

Plate 163. How it all begins. Father and son standing at the end of a platform watching the arrivals and departures. 'Britannia' Class loco No. 70024 *Vulcan* backs slowly down from Holyhead Depot to head an up 'Irish Mail'. On the opposite platform Black 5 No. 44844 prepares to head the first relief mail.

E. N. Kneale

◁ Plate 162. 'Jubilee' Class No. 45563 *Australia* blasts her way out of Holyhead and past the sheds where two Black 5s await their turn to come off and run down light engine to the terminus.

E. N. Kneale

Plate 164. B.R. 'Britannia' Pacific No. 70004 *William Shakespeare* hauls a relief 'Irish Mail' up the steep gradient out of Holyhead.

B. A. Wynne

Plate 166. 'Jubilee' Class 4–6–0 No. 45667 *Jellicoe* moves off Holyhead Shed on a bright winter's afternoon.

B. A. Wynne

◁ *Plate 165.* Sunlight and shadow on the front end of an ex works 'Coronation' Pacific No. 46246 *City of Manchester* at Holyhead.

B. A. Wynne

Plate 167. B.R. Pacific No. 70042 *Lord Roberts* waits for the signal to allow her out on to the main line, later to head a mixed parcel train towards Chester.

B. A. Wynne

Plate 169. Holyhead Shed staff are seen busy cleaning and polishing two Black 5s that had been allocated to be Royal engine and stand-by engine. Outside the shed in bright sunlight is Black 5 No. 44821 and inside the Shed No. 45247.

E. N. Kneale

Plate 168. Final polishing for the front bogies of a Royal engine on Holyhead Shed, in the form of Black 5 No. 45247.

E. N. Kneale

Plate 170. Stanier Pacific No. 46228 *Duchess of Rutland* waits on Holyhead for her turn of duty with the 'Emerald Isle Express'.

E. N. Kneale

Pre-Nationalisation

Plate 171. Not many years after the L.M.S. came into being, it was decided to have a trial run between London and Holyhead (263 miles non-stop). The train was hauled by a 'Claughton' Class loco, and departed from Euston at 8.15 a.m. and arrived in Holyhead at 2.03 p.m. The photograph shows driver David Noble and fireman William Williams (extreme left and right on footplate), and the guard for this run was a goods guard from Willesden, who had taken the job at short notice. The young fireman on the footplate, and a driver standing on the platform, were part of a larger interested party that greeted the arrival.

J. Clay

Plate 172. 'Royal Scot' No. 6116 *Irish Guardsman*, with sanding gear in use, loses her feet just for a moment as she climbs the heavy but short gradient out of Holyhead Station with an up 'Irish Mail'. The unrebuilt 'Royal Scots' had their work cut out with the up and down 'Irish Mails'. Fifteen and sixteen coaches fully loaded were commonplace, but they coped admirably with them.

H. A. Coulter

Plate 173. 'Jubilee' Class No. 5560 *Prince Edward Island* trundles slowly on to Holyhead turntable.

H. A. Coulter

Plate 174. 'Royal Scot' No. 6159 *The Royal Air Force* being prepared for one of the London expresses on Holyhead Shed. The crosshead vacuum pump and bogie brakes can be clearly seen, both of these components being subsequently removed.

H. A. Coulter

Plate 176. 'Royal Scot' No. 6163 seen here un-named, poses with drivers, firemen and shed staff of Holyhead outside their shed. The white substance on the boiler cladding is a mixture of bath brick and oil, which was used to clean up the paint-work. This locomotive was later named *Civil Service Rifleman*.

H. A. Coulter

Plate 175. 'Royal Scot' No. 6163 *Civil Service Rifleman* on Holyhead Shed being oiled prior to working an express train to London.

H. A. Coulter

Plate 177. Some of Holyhead's shed staff proudly display two famous headboards. Both modern and traditional headgear is being worn by some of the men.

E. N. Kneale

Plate 178. A Holyhead driver places the headboard of 'The Emerald Isle Express' in position on the front end of Stanier Pacific No. 46228 *Duchess of Rutland*.

E. N. Kneale